EGG!

First edition

Wood, A. J., 1960 –
    Egg!: a dozen eggs, what will they be?
Unfold each page and you will see! / written by
A. J. Wood; illustrated by Stella Stilwell.
        p. cm.
    Summary: The reader must unfold the
page to discover what kind of creature hatches
out of twelve different eggs.
    ISBN 0-316-81616-7
    1. Reproduction — Juvenile literature.
2. Eggs — Juvenile literature.
3. Toy and movable books — Specimens.
[1. Eggs. 2. Reproduction. 3. Toy and movable books.]
I. Stilwell, Stella, ill. II. Title.
QP251.5.W66   1993
591.3'9 — dc20   92-17930

10 9 8 7 6 5 4 3 2 1

A TEMPLAR BOOK
Devised and produced by The Templar Company plc,
Pippbrook Mill, London Road, Dorking, Surrey RH4 1JE, England.

Published simultaneously in Canada
by Little, Brown & Company (Canada) Limited

Printed in Singapore

EGG!

Written by A. J. Wood
Illustrated by Stella Stilwell

Little, Brown and Company
Boston   Toronto   London

1

This egg belongs
to the world's largest bird.
It lives on the plains of Africa,
where it feeds on insects and berries.
It can run as fast as a zebra, racing on its
long legs at speeds of up to 40 miles per hour.
Its babies can run almost as soon as they hatch.
But it will take them 18 months to grow to their
full height of 8 feet. Do you know whose
egg this is? Pull open the fold to reveal
the answer, and you'll also find four of
this creature's relatives. Can you
guess what they all have
in common?

 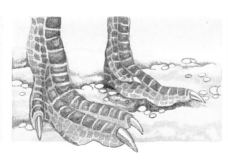 

2

These eggs aren't at all like birds' eggs. They are laid underwater and have a sac of jelly to protect the tiny baby inside, instead of a hard outer shell. Each egg eventually hatches into a fishlike creature called a tadpole. Over several weeks the tadpole grows and changes shape through a process called metamorphosis. Do you know what it eventually changes into? Open the fold and you will find out. You will also see some other creatures that produce eggs similar to this one.

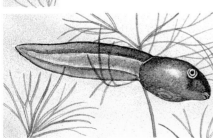

3

You would not
want to get too close to the
mother of these eggs! She is one of the
largest and most dangerous reptiles on Earth,
and spends most of her time swimming in rivers
and lakes, hunting for other animals to eat. She
comes ashore to sunbathe and to lay her eggs.
These are buried in a pit on the riverbank, which
the mother will guard until the babies hatch,
carrying them to safety in her huge jaws. What
is the name of this giant reptile? Open the
page to learn the answer and you'll also
find two of this creature's
close relatives.

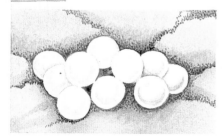

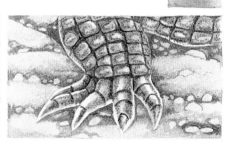

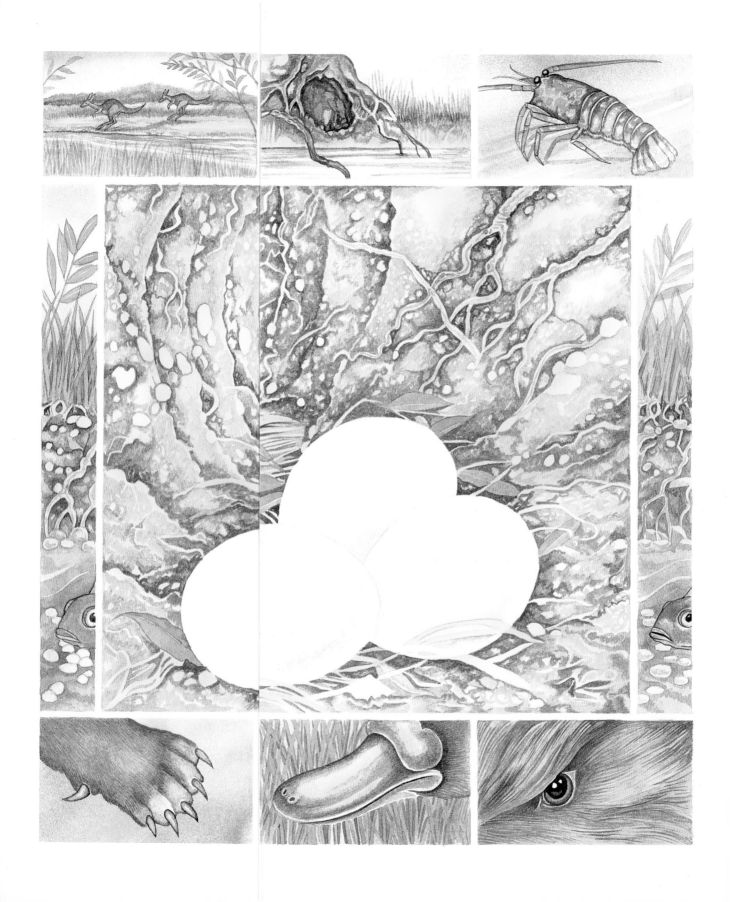

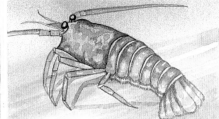

4

These eggs belong
to one of the world's most
curious creatures. You would have to go
all the way to Australia to find it, for this
animal lives nowhere else in the world. Its
body is covered in soft fur like most mammals,
but it has webbed feet and an extraordinary
birdlike beak. It spends most of of its time
swimming around underwater in search of fish,
shrimps, and frogs to eat. It lays its eggs in
a long burrow dug into the riverbank and
feeds its babies milk. Can you guess its
name? Unfold the page to see
if you are right.

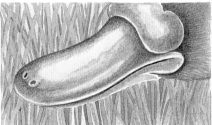

5

The tiny
eggs on these leaves were
laid by some of the world's most
colorful insects. Their young do not look
anything like the adults when they hatch.
Instead, they look rather like brightly colored
worms. They have to go through another stage
of growing, called a chrysalis, before they become
winged insects like their parents. This growth
process is known as metamorphosis.
Can you guess the names of these
insects and their young? Open
the page to see if you
are right.

EGG

CATERPILLAR

PUSS MOTH

PUSS MOTH
CATERPILLAR

PEACOCK
BUTTERFLY

PEACOCK
CATERPILLAR

CHRYSALIS

BUTTERFLY

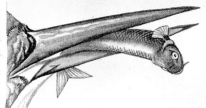

6

These eggs
belong to a colorful bird
that lives by rivers and ponds.
The eggs are laid in a burrow, dug
by their mother in a sandy riverbank.
They will hatch after about three weeks into
tiny chicks that will learn to be expert flyers
like their parents, speeding low over the water like
shining blue and orange bullets in search
of fish. Can you guess the name of this
feathery fisherman? Open the fold and you
will find the answer, along with four
other birds that also lay their
eggs underground.

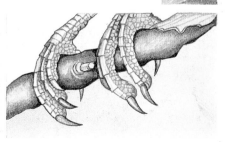

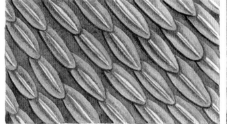  

7

Many people
are frightened by the mother of
these eggs and her hundreds of relatives.
She has a long scaly body, bright beady eyes,
and a forked tongue that she flicks in and
out to "smell" the air. Every spring she lays a
clutch of up to 50 eggs that hatch after about 2
months. The babies will soon be slithering through
the undergrowth like their parents, hunting
for mice and frogs to eat. Can you guess
the name of this familiar reptile? Unfold
the page to find the answer and you
will also see four other reptiles that
lay eggs like this.

 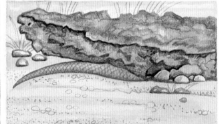 

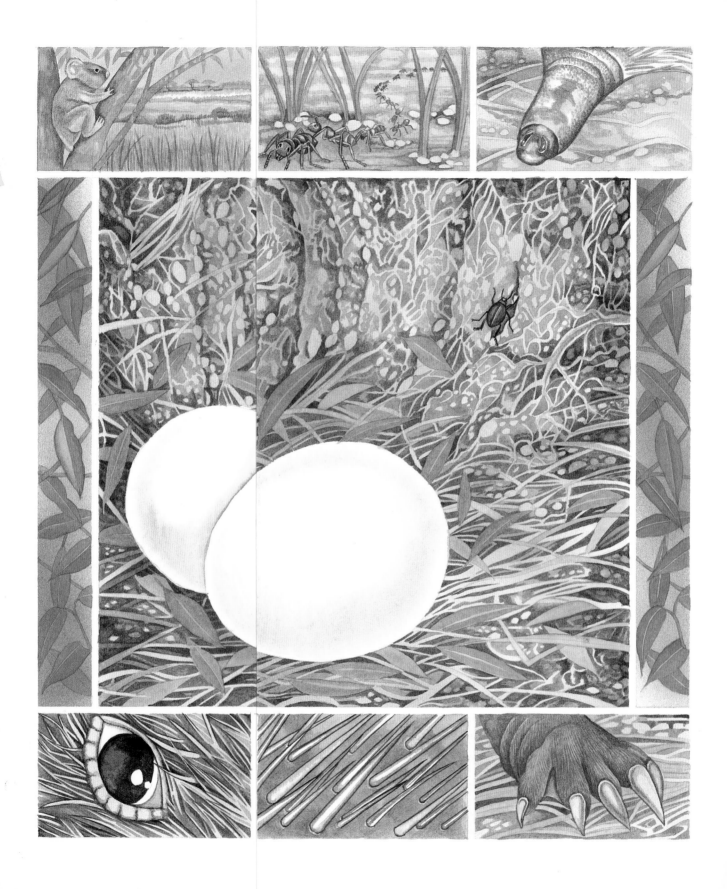

  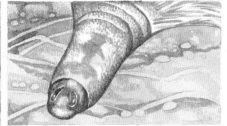

8

The mother of
this egg is the only other
egg-laying mammal aside from the
platypus. It, too, lives in Australia, where
it feeds on ants and other small insects,
catching them with the help of its pointed
snout and long, sticky tongue. Its baby hatches
from a leathery-shelled egg laid on the mother's
belly. It will take many months for the baby to
grow the protective spines that cover the
bodies of its parents. Can you guess its
name? Unfold the page and you will
find both members of this
unusual animal family.

 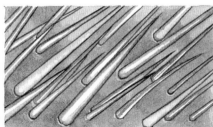 

  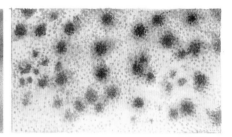

9

This strange capsule
is an egg case, protecting
the growing baby of a sea-dwelling
fish. You can sometimes find the empty
egg cases washed up on the beach. They
are known as mermaid's purses. This young
fish will soon hatch and begin hunting its food
of worms, mollusks, and other fish among the
ocean waters. It is a member of a big family
that contains some of the most dangerous
of all fishes. Do you know what it is?
Open the page to find out and
you'll discover four other
fish that lay eggs.

 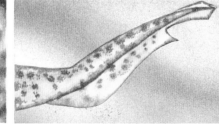 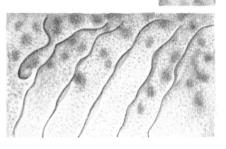

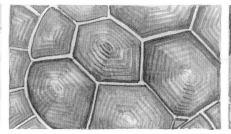

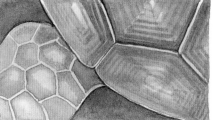

10

The mother of
these eggs spends almost all
her life in the water. Every few years
she will return to the place where she was
born to lay her own eggs. She will bury these
deep in the sand of the beach before returning to
her home in the sea. The babies will hatch after
several months to look like miniature versions
of their parents, with a hard shell covering
their backs. Can you guess the name of this
sea reptile? Unfold the page to find the
answer and you'll also discover
four of this creature's
close relatives.

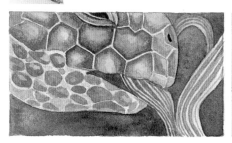

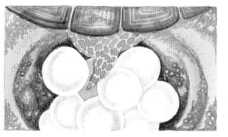

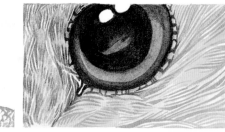

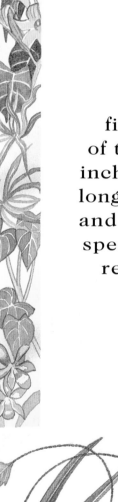

11

This tiny
nest belongs to one of the
world's smallest birds. You would
find it built high up among the branches
of the rainforest. Its owner measures only 3
inches from the tip of its tail to the end of its
long beak. It uses this beak to feed on insects
and flowers, licking up their nectar with its
special brush-tipped tongue. Like its many
relatives, this bird can hover in midair,
beating its tiny wings over 50 times
each second. Do you know its
name? Open the page
to find out.

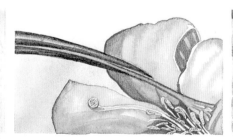

SWORD-BILLED HUMMINGBIRD

LUCIFER HUMMINGBIRD

HERMIT HUMMINGBIRD

SICKLEBILL HUMMINGBIRD

VELVET-BREASTED HUMMINGBIRD

12

This huge egg
belongs to a creature that
grew to the size of a small truck.
To find one, you would have to travel back
in time, to over 65 million years ago. Although
this giant had ferocious horns and huge claws
on its feet, it ate only plants. These creatures are
now extinct but the remains of some have been
preserved in Earth's rocks as fossils. Can
you guess whose egg this is? Open the page
to find out and you'll also discover some
other creatures that lived on Earth
many millions of
years ago.

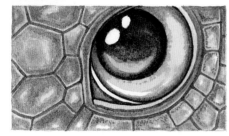  

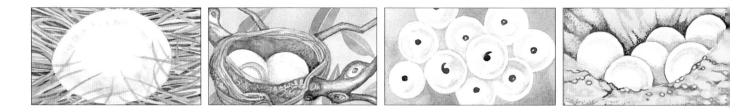

How big?

Here you can find out the sizes of all the eggs in this book, from the smallest to the biggest!

Puss moth — $1/10$ inch

Frog — $1/4$ inch

Hummingbird — $1/2$ inch

Spiny Anteater — $3/4$ inch

Platypus — $3/4$ inch

Kingfisher — 1 inch

Corn Snake — $1^1/4$ inches

Green Turtle — $2^3/4$ inches

Sandy Dogfish Shark — 3 inches

Crocodile — $3^1/2$ inches

Ostrich — 8 inches

Triceratops Dinosaur — approx. 10 inches